I0490734

Table Of Contents

As a developer, you might be wondering why full-stack Shopify app development is important. The answer is simple - it allows you to create a complete solution that covers all aspects of the Shopify platform, from the user interface to cloud integration. By developing a full-stack Shopify app, you can create a seamless experience for both the store owners and their customers.

One of the benefits of full-stack Shopify app development is that it allows you to create a custom user interface that meets the specific needs of the business. With full-stack development, you have complete control over the design and functionality of the app. This means that you can create a unique user experience that sets your app apart from the competition.

Another benefit of full-stack Shopify app development is that it allows you to integrate with other third-party services seamlessly. For example, if the business uses a third-party shipping provider, you can integrate their services into the app, making the shipping process more efficient for the business and its customers. Additionally, you can integrate with cloud services like AWS or Google Cloud, which can help improve the scalability and reliability of the app.

Full-stack Shopify app development also allows you to create a more scalable and maintainable app. By using a full-stack approach, you can ensure that the app is well-architected and follows best practices for scalability and maintainability. This means that the app can grow and evolve over time without becoming too complex or difficult to maintain.

In conclusion, full-stack Shopify app development is important because it allows you to create a complete solution that covers all aspects of the Shopify platform. By developing a full-stack app, you can create a seamless experience for both the store owners and their customers. Additionally, full-stack development allows you to create a custom user interface, integrate with third-party services, and create a more scalable and maintainable app.

Who this Book is For

If you're a developer looking to expand your skillset and dive into the world of full-stack Shopify app development, then this book is for you. Whether you're a seasoned developer or just starting out, this handbook will provide you with the knowledge and tools you need to build high-quality Shopify apps that integrate seamlessly with the platform.

This book is specifically designed for developers who are interested in building Shopify apps from the ground up. We'll cover everything from user interface design to cloud integration, so you'll have a comprehensive understanding of what it takes to build a successful app on the Shopify platform.

We'll also dive into the technical aspects of Shopify app development, including the Shopify API, webhooks, and the Shopify CLI. This book is perfect for developers who are already familiar with these technologies, or those who are looking to learn more about them in the context of Shopify app development.

In addition to technical knowledge, this book will also provide you with practical tips and best practices for building Shopify apps that are user-friendly, scalable, and secure. You'll learn how to design user interfaces that are both aesthetically pleasing and functional, and how to optimize your app's performance for the best possible user experience.

Ultimately, this book is for developers who are passionate about creating high-quality Shopify apps that add value to merchants and their customers. If you're ready to take your Shopify app development skills to the next level, then this handbook is the perfect resource for you.

What You'll Learn

In this subchapter, we will discuss what you can expect to learn from reading "Full-Stack Shopify App Development: The Developer's Handbook." This book is specifically designed to help developers master the art and science of building full-stack Shopify apps.

First, you will learn how to create a user interface that is both visually appealing and highly functional. This involves understanding the principles of good design, as well as the technical aspects of creating a responsive and intuitive interface.

Next, you will dive into the world of Shopify app development, learning how to build custom apps that integrate with the Shopify platform. You will learn how to use the Shopify API to access and manipulate data, as well as how to create custom functionality that extends beyond the standard features of Shopify.

As you progress through the book, you will also learn how to work with various cloud platforms, including AWS, Azure, and Google Cloud. This will enable you to create apps that are highly scalable, flexible, and secure, as well as to take advantage of the latest cloud technologies and innovations.

In addition, you will learn how to optimize your app for performance, ensuring that it runs smoothly and efficiently even under heavy traffic loads. You will also learn how to debug and troubleshoot your app, as well as how to test it thoroughly to ensure that it meets the highest standards of quality and reliability.

Overall, "Full-Stack Shopify App Development: The Developer's Handbook" is an essential resource for any developer who wants to master the art of building full-stack Shopify apps. Whether you are a seasoned pro or just starting out, this book will provide you with the knowledge and skills you need to succeed in this exciting and rapidly growing field.

Prerequisites

Prerequisites

Before diving into full-stack Shopify app development, it is important to have a solid foundation in web development. This includes proficiency in HTML, CSS, and JavaScript, as well as experience with at least one server-side language such as Ruby on Rails or Node.js.

Additionally, familiarity with Shopify's API is crucial for building successful Shopify apps. This includes understanding the various endpoints and data structures, as well as authentication and authorization processes. Developers should also be familiar with OAuth 2.0 as it is used extensively in Shopify's API.

In terms of tools and frameworks, developers should have experience working with popular front-end frameworks such as React or Vue.js. They should also be comfortable using popular version control systems such as Git, as well as package managers such as npm or Yarn.

It is also important to have a basic understanding of cloud computing and deployment, as Shopify apps are hosted on the cloud. Familiarity with cloud computing providers such as Amazon Web Services or Google Cloud Platform is beneficial.

Finally, as full-stack Shopify app development involves both front-end and back-end development, developers should have experience working with databases such as SQL or NoSQL, as well as server-side frameworks such as Ruby on Rails or Node.js.

Overall, full-stack Shopify app development requires a diverse set of skills and experience. Developers should have a strong foundation in web development, as well as experience with Shopify's API and front-end frameworks. Additionally, familiarity with cloud computing and deployment, as well as server-side frameworks and databases, is crucial for building successful Shopify apps.

Getting Started with Shopify App Development

Setting up Your Shopify Development Environment

As a developer, setting up your Shopify development environment is an essential step in building full-stack Shopify apps. This process involves installing tools and configuring your workspace to ensure that you have everything you need to create, test, and deploy your applications.

The first step in setting up your development environment is to install the necessary tools. These include a code editor, a version control system, and a local development server. Popular code editors for Shopify development include Visual Studio Code, Atom, and Sublime Text. Version control systems such as Git are also essential in managing your code changes and collaborating with other developers.

Once you have installed your tools, you need to configure your workspace to ensure that you can work efficiently. This involves setting up your code editor, installing necessary plugins and extensions, and creating a local development server. For example, with Visual Studio Code, you can install the Shopify Theme Kit extension to manage your Shopify themes and upload your changes to the Shopify platform.

Another crucial step in setting up your development environment is to create a Shopify development store. This allows you to test your applications in a sandbox environment without affecting your live store. You can create a development store by signing up for a Shopify partner account and accessing the developer dashboard.

Finally, you need to integrate your development environment with the Shopify platform to ensure that you can build full-stack Shopify apps. This involves using Shopify APIs and SDKs to interact with the Shopify platform and access data and services such as product information, orders, and payments. You can also use cloud integration services such as AWS, Google Cloud, and Microsoft Azure to host your applications and ensure scalability and reliability.

In conclusion, setting up your Shopify development environment is an essential step in building full-stack Shopify apps. It involves installing tools, configuring your workspace, creating a development store, and integrating your environment with the Shopify platform. By following these steps, you can ensure that you have everything you need to create, test, and deploy your applications efficiently.

Understanding the Shopify API

Understanding the Shopify API is essential for any developer looking to develop full-stack Shopify apps. The Shopify API provides developers with the necessary tools to create powerful and efficient apps that can integrate with Shopify, providing a seamless user experience for customers.

The Shopify API is a RESTful API, which means that it is built on the principles of Representational State Transfer (REST). This architecture allows developers to access and manipulate resources through a set of HTTP methods, such as GET, POST, PUT, and DELETE. These methods enable developers to retrieve data, add new data, update existing data, and delete data.

The Shopify API is divided into several parts, including the Admin API, the Storefront API, and the GraphQL API. The Admin API is used to manage store data, such as products, orders, and customers. The Storefront API is used to retrieve store data, such as products and collections, to display on the frontend of the app. The GraphQL API is a powerful tool that allows developers to query and mutate data in a single request.

To use the Shopify API, developers must create a Shopify Partner account and register their app. Once the app is registered, developers can obtain an API key and API secret key, which are used to authenticate requests to the API.

Developers can use various programming languages and frameworks to interact with the Shopify API, such as Ruby on Rails, Python, Node.js, and React. Shopify also provides SDKs and libraries for various programming languages, which can make it easier for developers to work with the API.

In conclusion, understanding the Shopify API is crucial for developing full-stack Shopify apps. The API provides developers with the tools they need to create powerful and efficient apps that can integrate seamlessly with Shopify. By using the Shopify API, developers can access and manipulate store data, creating a better user experience for customers.

Basic Shopify App Development Concepts

Basic Shopify App Development Concepts

Shopify is a powerful e-commerce platform that allows businesses to create an online store and sell products to customers around the world. With Shopify, developers can create custom apps that extend the functionality of the platform and provide additional features to merchants.

If you're interested in full-stack Shopify app development, it's important to understand the basic concepts and terminology that are used in the Shopify ecosystem. Here are some key concepts that you should be familiar with:

1. API: Shopify's API (Application Programming Interface) is a set of rules and protocols that developers can use to interact with the Shopify platform. The API allows developers to create custom apps that can read and write data to a Shopify store.

2. Webhooks: Webhooks are a way for Shopify to send real-time notifications to your app when certain events occur, such as when a new order is placed or when a product is updated. Your app can use webhooks to trigger actions or update data in response to these events.

3. Shopify App Store: The Shopify App Store is a marketplace where merchants can browse and install apps that add new functionality to their stores. If you want to distribute your app to Shopify merchants, you'll need to submit it to the App Store for review.

4. OAuth: OAuth is a protocol that allows users to grant your app access to their Shopify store without giving you their login credentials. When a user installs your app, they'll be prompted to authorize it using OAuth.

5. Embedded apps: Embedded apps are apps that are built into the Shopify admin interface. These apps can provide a seamless user experience by integrating directly with the Shopify interface.

By understanding these basic concepts, you'll be well on your way to developing full-stack Shopify apps that provide value to merchants and help them grow their businesses. In the next chapter, we'll dive deeper into the Shopify API and explore some of the ways that you can use it to build custom apps.

Front-End Development with Shopify

Introduction to Front-End Development

Introduction to Front-End Development

Front-end development is the process of creating the user interface and experience of a website or application. It involves designing and building the parts of a website that users interact with, such as buttons, menus, forms, and content.

In the context of full-stack Shopify app development, front-end development is an essential part of the process. Creating a user-friendly and visually appealing interface is crucial to the success of any Shopify app. It can help increase user engagement and drive sales for merchants.

Front-end developers use a variety of technologies and tools to create the visual elements of a website or application. Some of the most commonly used technologies include HTML, CSS, and JavaScript. HTML is used to define the structure of a web page, while CSS is used to control the layout and visual styling. JavaScript is used to add interactivity and dynamic functionality to a website or application.

In addition to these core technologies, front-end developers may also use frameworks such as React or Vue.js to create more complex interfaces. These frameworks provide pre-built components and tools that can help speed up development and improve code quality.

Another important aspect of front-end development is responsive design. With more and more users accessing websites and applications on mobile devices, it's essential to ensure that the interface is optimized for different screen sizes and resolutions. This involves using techniques such as fluid layouts, flexible images, and media queries to adapt the interface to different devices.

In conclusion, front-end development is a critical part of full-stack Shopify app development. It involves designing and building the user interface and experience of a website or application using technologies such as HTML, CSS, and JavaScript. Front-end developers may also use frameworks such as React or Vue.js to speed up development and improve code quality. Responsive design is also an essential aspect of front-end development, ensuring that the interface is optimized for different devices.

Shopify Theme Development

Shopify Theme Development

Shopify is a powerful platform that enables businesses to create and manage their online stores with ease. However, the default Shopify themes may not always meet the specific needs of every business. This is where Shopify theme development comes in.

Shopify theme development involves creating custom themes that better reflect a business's brand and meet its unique requirements. With theme development, developers can create a visually appealing and user-friendly online store that is tailored to the needs of the business.

Developers can either create a new theme from scratch or customize an existing theme to fit the business's needs. Shopify's theme development tools provide developers with a range of options to create themes, including HTML, CSS, and Liquid.

HTML is used to create the structure of the theme, while CSS is used to style the theme's layout and design. Liquid is Shopify's templating language, which allows developers to add dynamic content to the theme, such as product images, descriptions, and prices.

With Shopify's theme development tools, developers can create themes that are responsive and optimized for mobile devices. This is important, as more and more consumers are using their mobile devices to shop online.

In addition to creating visually appealing themes, developers can also integrate various Shopify apps into the theme to provide additional functionality to the online store. This can include features such as social media integration, advanced search options, and personalized recommendations.

Overall, Shopify theme development is an essential aspect of full-stack Shopify app development. It enables businesses to create a unique and engaging online store that better reflects their brand and meets their specific needs. With Shopify's theme development tools, developers can create visually appealing and user-friendly themes that are optimized for mobile devices and integrate various Shopify apps to provide additional functionality.

Shopify Liquid Templating

Shopify Liquid Templating

Shopify Liquid Templating is the backbone of Shopify development. It is a templating language developed by Shopify, which is used to build the front-end of Shopify stores. Shopify Liquid Templating is a powerful tool that allows developers to create dynamic, responsive, and customizable web pages in Shopify.

The language is based on Ruby and provides a simple syntax for developers to build templates. It is a flexible language that can be used to create custom pages, blogs, and product pages. The language allows developers to create reusable snippets, which can be used across multiple templates.

When building a Shopify app, developers need to understand Shopify Liquid Templating. The language allows developers to create custom templates that can be used to display data from the Shopify API. Shopify Liquid Templating is used to create templates for product pages, collections, blogs, and other pages on a Shopify store.

One of the key benefits of Shopify Liquid Templating is its flexibility. Developers can use the language to build custom templates that match the design and branding of the Shopify store. The language also allows developers to create reusable snippets, which can be used across multiple templates. This makes it easier to maintain and update the codebase.

Another benefit of Shopify Liquid Templating is its integration with the Shopify API. The language allows developers to access data from the Shopify API and display it on the front-end of the store. This makes it easier to create dynamic and responsive pages that display up-to-date information.

In conclusion, Shopify Liquid Templating is a powerful tool for Shopify developers. It allows developers to create custom templates, reusable snippets, and dynamic pages that integrate with the Shopify API. As a developer, it is important to understand Shopify Liquid Templating to build effective and efficient Shopify apps.

Styling Your Shopify App with CSS

Styling Your Shopify App with CSS

As a developer, you understand that user experience is essential in any application. The same is true for Shopify apps. The appearance of your app can impact how users interact with it, and ultimately, whether they continue to use it.

To make your Shopify app visually appealing, you need to style it using Cascading Style Sheets (CSS). CSS is a language that defines how HTML elements should look. It enables you to customize the appearance of your app, including fonts, colors, and layout.

In this section, we'll discuss how you can style your Shopify app with CSS.

1. Create a CSS file

The first step is to create a CSS file for your app. You can do this by creating a new file in your app's directory and naming it "style.css." Alternatively, you can add a link to an existing CSS file in your app.

2. Use CSS selectors

CSS selectors are used to target specific HTML elements and apply style rules to them. For example, to change the color of all H1 headings in your app, you can use the following selector:

```
h1 {
color: red;
}
```

3. Use CSS properties

CSS properties are used to define the values of style rules. For example, to change the font size of all paragraph elements in your app, you can use the following property:

```
p {
font-size: 16px;
}
```

4. Use CSS classes

CSS classes are used to apply style rules to specific HTML elements. You can add a class to an HTML element by using the "class" attribute. For example:

This is a paragraph.

You can then target that class in your CSS file to apply style rules to all elements with that class:

```
.my-class {
color: blue;
}
```

5. Use CSS frameworks

CSS frameworks are pre-written CSS code that you can use to style your app. Popular frameworks include Bootstrap and Foundation. These frameworks provide a set of pre-defined CSS classes and properties that you can use to create a consistent and professional-looking app.

In conclusion, styling your Shopify app with CSS can enhance the user experience and make your app stand out. By following the tips outlined above, you can create a visually appealing app that users will love to use.

JavaScript and jQuery in Shopify

JavaScript and jQuery in Shopify

JavaScript and jQuery are two powerful tools that can be used to enhance the functionality and user experience of a Shopify app. In this subchapter, we will explore how to use these tools effectively in a Shopify app development project.

JavaScript is a programming language that is used to create interactive and dynamic web pages. It can be used to add functionality to a Shopify app, such as creating pop-up windows or adding animations to a page. jQuery is a JavaScript library that simplifies the process of using JavaScript by providing a set of pre-written functions.

One of the most common uses of JavaScript and jQuery in Shopify app development is to create custom forms. Shopify's built-in form builder is limited in functionality, so developers often turn to JavaScript and jQuery to create more complex forms. This can include features such as custom validation, conditional logic, and dynamic form fields.

Another use for JavaScript and jQuery in Shopify app development is to create custom product pages. Shopify's default product pages are functional but may not meet the needs of all merchants. By using JavaScript and jQuery, developers can create custom product pages that include features such as image zoom, product sliders, and tabbed content.

JavaScript and jQuery can also be used to create custom checkout pages. Shopify's default checkout pages are simple and functional, but may not meet the needs of all merchants. By using JavaScript and jQuery, developers can create custom checkout pages that include features such as custom shipping rates, custom payment methods, and custom order summaries.

In conclusion, JavaScript and jQuery are powerful tools that can be used to enhance the functionality and user experience of a Shopify app. By using these tools effectively, developers can create custom forms, product pages, and checkout pages that meet the unique needs of their clients.

Back-End Development with Shopify

Introduction to Back-End Development

Introduction to Back-End Development

In the world of full-stack Shopify app development, back-end development is an essential aspect that cannot be ignored. It is the backbone of the entire application, responsible for processing, storing, and managing data that powers the app's dynamic user interface. In this chapter, we'll explore the basics of back-end development and its role in building successful Shopify apps.

Back-end development is the part of web development that focuses on the server-side of the application. It involves writing code that runs on the server, rather than on the client-side browser. The back-end code handles data storage, communication between the server and client, and the overall functionality of the application.

Back-end development requires a different set of skills from front-end development. While front-end development focuses on designing the user interface and user experience, back-end development deals with the logic and functionality of the application. Developers working on the back-end of an application need to have a solid understanding of how databases work, how to write efficient code, and how to secure data.

One of the essential aspects of back-end development is data storage. Every application needs to store data, and back-end developers need to decide which type of database to use. The most common types of databases used in back-end development are relational databases like MySQL and PostgreSQL and NoSQL databases like MongoDB and Cassandra.

Back-end developers also need to be familiar with APIs (Application Programming Interfaces). APIs are a way for two applications to communicate with each other. In the context of full-stack Shopify app development, APIs are used to communicate with Shopify's API to retrieve data and perform actions on behalf of the user.

In conclusion, back-end development is a critical component of full-stack Shopify app development. It's responsible for managing data, communication between the server and client, and the overall functionality of the application. Back-end developers need to have a solid understanding of databases, APIs, and how to write efficient and secure code. With this knowledge, you can build robust and scalable Shopify apps that provide an exceptional user experience.

Shopify App Architecture

As a developer, understanding the Shopify App Architecture is essential in creating full-stack Shopify apps that are both efficient and effective. Shopify App Architecture refers to the framework or structure of a Shopify app that determines how the app interacts with the Shopify platform and other third-party services.

The Shopify App Architecture is divided into three main components: the front-end, the back-end, and the API. The front-end is responsible for the user interface and experience of the app, while the back-end handles the business logic and data storage. The API is the intermediary between the front-end and back-end and enables communication between the Shopify platform and the app.

The front-end of a Shopify app is typically built using HTML, CSS, and JavaScript. Shopify provides developers with a JavaScript library called the Shopify App Bridge, which allows them to integrate their app with the Shopify platform seamlessly. The Shopify App Bridge also provides a set of UI components that developers can use to build their app's user interface.

The back-end of a Shopify app is where the business logic of the app resides. Developers can choose to build the back-end using any programming language of their choice, such as Ruby on Rails, Node.js, or PHP. The back-end is responsible for processing data and performing actions on behalf of the user.

The API is the glue that holds the front-end and back-end together. The Shopify API provides developers with a set of endpoints that they can use to interact with the Shopify platform. These endpoints allow developers to retrieve data from the Shopify platform, create and modify products, orders, and customers, and perform other actions.

In conclusion, understanding the Shopify App Architecture is essential for any developer looking to create full-stack Shopify apps. By knowing the different components of the architecture and how they work together, developers can create apps that are both efficient and effective. With the right tools and skills, developers can build apps that provide a seamless user experience and integrate seamlessly with the Shopify platform.

Shopify App Development with Ruby on Rails

Shopify App Development with Ruby on Rails

Shopify is a cloud-based e-commerce platform that offers a range of services to help businesses sell their products online. One of the key features of Shopify is the ability to extend its functionality through apps. Shopify apps can be created using various programming languages, including Ruby on Rails.

Ruby on Rails is a popular web application framework that provides developers with a set of tools for building web applications quickly and easily. It is an open-source framework that is built on the Ruby programming language. Ruby on Rails is known for its simplicity, flexibility, and ease of use.

When it comes to Shopify app development, Ruby on Rails offers several advantages. First, Ruby on Rails is a mature and well-established framework with a large community of developers. This means that there are plenty of resources available to help developers get started with Shopify app development using Ruby on Rails.

Second, Ruby on Rails is a highly productive framework. It provides developers with many built-in features that can help them build Shopify apps quickly and easily. For example, Ruby on Rails has a robust database layer that makes it easy to store and retrieve data from Shopify.

Third, Ruby on Rails is highly customizable. It allows developers to create custom modules and plugins that can be easily integrated into Shopify. This makes it easy to add new features and functionality to a Shopify store.

Finally, Ruby on Rails is highly scalable. It can handle large volumes of traffic and can be easily scaled up or down as needed. This makes it a great choice for building Shopify apps that need to handle a large number of users or transactions.

In summary, Ruby on Rails is an excellent choice for Shopify app development. It offers a range of benefits, including productivity, customization, scalability, and a large community of developers. If you are a developer looking to build Shopify apps, Ruby on Rails is definitely worth considering.

Shopify Webhooks and APIs

Shopify Webhooks and APIs

As a developer, understanding webhooks and APIs is crucial for building a full-stack Shopify app. Webhooks are a way for Shopify to communicate with your app in real-time, notifying it of any changes that occur within the store. APIs, on the other hand, allow your app to interact with Shopify's platform, accessing and manipulating data to provide a seamless user experience.

Webhooks

Webhooks are essentially triggers that are fired when specific events occur within a Shopify store. For example, a webhook may be triggered when a new order is placed, a product is updated, or a customer is created. Once a webhook is triggered, Shopify sends a payload of data to your app's URL, allowing your app to respond accordingly.

To set up webhooks for your app, you'll need to create a webhook subscription within the Shopify admin panel. This involves specifying the event(s) you want to listen for and the URL of your app's webhook endpoint. Once your subscription is created, Shopify will send a test webhook to ensure that your app is correctly configured to receive them.

APIs

Shopify's APIs allow your app to interact with the platform, accessing and manipulating data to provide a seamless user experience. The Shopify API is a RESTful API that utilizes HTTP requests to send and receive data in JSON format. By using the Shopify API, your app can read and write data to a store, including products, collections, customers, orders, and more.

To use the Shopify API, you'll need to authenticate your app using an API key and secret. Once authenticated, you can make API requests to read, create, update, and delete data within a store. For example, you might use the API to create a new product, update a customer's information, or fulfill an order.

Conclusion

Webhooks and APIs are essential tools for building a full-stack Shopify app. By leveraging webhooks, your app can respond in real-time to changes within a store, providing a seamless user experience. APIs, on the other hand, allow your app to interact with Shopify's platform, accessing and manipulating data to provide a rich set of features. As a developer, it's important to understand these concepts and how to use them effectively to build a successful Shopify app.

Shopify App Security

Shopify App Security

As a developer, it is crucial to prioritize security when developing Shopify apps. With the growing number of cyber attacks and data breaches, customers are becoming more aware of the importance of securing their personal information. Therefore, it is important to ensure that your Shopify app is secure to protect both your customers and your business.

One of the first steps in securing your Shopify app is to use secure coding practices. This means using best practices when writing your code, such as input validation, output encoding, and error handling. Additionally, you should use secure coding frameworks, such as Ruby on Rails, to ensure that your code is secure.

Another important aspect of Shopify app security is authentication and authorization. You should authenticate and authorize all users who access your app, and restrict access to sensitive data based on their level of authorization. This can be achieved through the use of access controls, such as role-based access controls, and two-factor authentication.

Encryption is also critical in securing Shopify apps. You should encrypt all sensitive data, such as customer information and payment details, both in transit and at rest. This can be achieved through the use of SSL/TLS protocols, hashing, and encryption algorithms.

Furthermore, it is important to regularly test your Shopify app for vulnerabilities. This includes running penetration tests, vulnerability assessments, and code reviews to identify potential weaknesses in your app. By regularly testing your app, you can identify and address potential security issues before they become a problem.

In conclusion, Shopify app security is essential for protecting both your customers and your business. By using secure coding practices, authentication and authorization, encryption, and regular testing, you can ensure that your Shopify app is secure and meets the highest standards of security. As a developer, it is important to prioritize security throughout the development process to build a trusted and reliable Shopify app.

Integrating Your Shopify App with Cloud Services

Introduction to Cloud Integration

Introduction to Cloud Integration

In the world of e-commerce, the integration of cloud services has become an essential part of the development process. Cloud integration is the process of connecting different applications and services over the cloud, allowing for seamless communication and data exchange between them. This technology has revolutionized the way businesses operate, allowing them to scale-up their operations, improve their efficiency, and reduce costs.

As a developer, understanding cloud integration is crucial in creating a full-stack Shopify app. Shopify is one of the most popular e-commerce platforms globally, and building a full-stack Shopify app requires a deep understanding of its API and how it can be integrated with cloud services. In this chapter, we will introduce you to the concept of cloud integration and explore its importance in full-stack Shopify app development.

Why is Cloud Integration Important?

Cloud integration offers a wide range of benefits to businesses, including seamless data exchange, scalability, flexibility, and reduced costs. With cloud integration, businesses can easily connect their different applications and services, allowing for real-time data exchange and collaboration. This means that businesses can operate more efficiently, reduce manual work, and make better decisions based on real-time data.

Another significant advantage of cloud integration is scalability. Cloud services offer businesses the flexibility to scale up or down their operations based on their needs. This means that businesses can quickly adapt to changing market conditions, expand their operations, or reduce costs by scaling down their operations.

Furthermore, cloud integration allows businesses to reduce costs by eliminating the need for physical servers, hardware, and software installations. This means that businesses can save money on IT infrastructure, maintenance, and support costs, allowing them to invest more in their core operations.

Conclusion

In conclusion, cloud integration is a crucial component in full-stack Shopify app development. Understanding cloud integration can help developers build more scalable, efficient, and cost-effective Shopify apps. By leveraging cloud services, businesses can improve their operations, reduce costs, and make better decisions based on real-time data. As a developer, it is essential to stay up-to-date with the latest cloud integration technologies to create high-quality Shopify apps that meet the needs of today's businesses.

Using Cloud Services in Shopify App Development

Using Cloud Services in Shopify App Development

Cloud services have transformed the way developers build and deploy applications. With the rise of cloud computing, developers can now leverage powerful computing resources and software tools to build apps that scale effortlessly. In this subchapter, we will discuss how you can use cloud services in your Shopify app development projects.

Benefits of Cloud Services in Shopify App Development

There are several benefits of using cloud services in Shopify app development. First and foremost, cloud services provide a scalable and flexible infrastructure that can handle high traffic and workload demands. This means that your app can grow and expand without worrying about infrastructure limitations.

Secondly, cloud services offer reliable and secure data storage, ensuring that your app's data is protected and always available. This is especially important for e-commerce apps that handle sensitive customer information.

Finally, cloud services offer a wide range of software tools and services that can help you build and deploy your app quickly and efficiently. From development environments to continuous integration and delivery tools, cloud services can streamline your development workflow and improve your app's quality.

Types of Cloud Services for Shopify App Development

There are several types of cloud services that you can use in Shopify app development. These include:

1. Infrastructure as a Service (IaaS): IaaS provides virtualized computing resources such as servers, storage, and networking. This allows you to build and deploy your app on a scalable and flexible infrastructure.

2. Platform as a Service (PaaS): PaaS provides a complete development environment that includes software tools, databases, and middleware. This allows you to focus on developing your app without worrying about managing infrastructure.

3. Software as a Service (SaaS): SaaS provides ready-to-use software applications that you can integrate into your app. This can save you time and effort in building certain features.

Examples of Cloud Services for Shopify App Development

There are several cloud services that you can use in Shopify app development. Some examples include:

1. Amazon Web Services (AWS): AWS provides a wide range of cloud services such as EC2, S3, and RDS. These services can be used to build and deploy scalable, secure, and reliable apps.

2. Google Cloud Platform (GCP): GCP provides a complete development environment that includes tools such as Google Cloud Storage, Google Cloud SQL, and Google Kubernetes Engine.

3. Microsoft Azure: Azure provides a wide range of cloud services such as Azure Virtual Machines, Azure Storage, and Azure App Service. These services can help you build and deploy your app quickly and efficiently.

Conclusion

In conclusion, cloud services can provide a range of benefits for Shopify app development. From scalability and flexibility to reliable data storage and software tools, cloud services can help you build high-quality apps that meet your customers' needs. By leveraging cloud services, you can streamline your development workflow and improve your app's performance and reliability.

Integrating Shopify with AWS

Integrating Shopify with AWS is a powerful way to enhance the functionality and scalability of your e-commerce application. AWS provides a comprehensive suite of cloud computing services that can help you build, deploy, and manage your Shopify app with ease.

In this subchapter, we will explore the various ways in which you can integrate Shopify with AWS, including:

1. Hosting your Shopify app on AWS: AWS provides a range of hosting options, including EC2 instances, Elastic Beanstalk, and Lambda functions. By hosting your Shopify app on AWS, you can benefit from its scalability and reliability, ensuring that your app can handle high traffic loads and operate smoothly even during peak periods.

2. Using AWS services for data storage: AWS provides a range of data storage services, including S3, RDS, and DynamoDB. By using these services, you can store and manage your Shopify app's data more efficiently, ensuring that it is secure, accessible, and easily scalable.

3. Leveraging AWS tools for analytics and monitoring: AWS provides powerful tools for monitoring and analyzing your Shopify app's performance, including CloudWatch and X-Ray. By using these tools, you can gain valuable insights into your app's behavior, identify performance bottlenecks, and optimize your app's performance.

4. Integrating Shopify with AWS APIs: AWS provides a range of APIs that can help you integrate Shopify with other AWS services, such as Amazon SNS, SQS, and SES. By leveraging these APIs, you can automate tasks, streamline workflows, and enhance the functionality of your Shopify app.

Integrating Shopify with AWS is an advanced topic that requires a deep understanding of both platforms. However, by mastering this skill, you can create powerful, scalable, and reliable e-commerce applications that can compete with the best in the industry.

In conclusion, integrating Shopify with AWS is a key skill for full-stack Shopify app developers. By leveraging the power of AWS, you can enhance your app's functionality, scalability, and reliability, ensuring that it can handle high traffic loads and operate smoothly even during peak periods. So, if you're serious about building top-quality Shopify apps, make sure to master this important skill.

Integrating Shopify with Google Cloud

Integrating Shopify with Google Cloud

Integrating Shopify with Google Cloud can offer several benefits to developers. Google Cloud is a flexible and scalable platform that can help you manage your Shopify store's data and applications. By integrating Shopify with Google Cloud, you can improve the performance and reliability of your store and make it easier to manage.

There are several ways to integrate Shopify with Google Cloud. One of the most popular methods is to use Google Cloud Storage to store your Shopify store's files. Google Cloud Storage is a powerful and scalable object storage service that can store and serve static assets like images, videos, and documents. By using Google Cloud Storage, you can reduce the load on your Shopify store's servers and improve the performance of your store.

Another way to integrate Shopify with Google Cloud is to use Google Cloud Functions to create serverless functions that can be triggered by Shopify events. Google Cloud Functions are lightweight and scalable, which makes them ideal for handling events like new orders, product updates, and customer sign-ups. By using Google Cloud Functions, you can build powerful workflows that can automate tasks like sending emails, updating databases, or triggering other Shopify apps.

You can also use Google Cloud Pub/Sub to build real-time data pipelines for your Shopify store. Google Cloud Pub/Sub is a messaging service that can handle large volumes of data and deliver it to multiple subscribers in real-time. By using Google Cloud Pub/Sub, you can build event-driven architectures that can respond to changes in your Shopify store's data and applications.

To integrate Shopify with Google Cloud, you'll need to have some knowledge of both platforms. You'll need to know how to set up a Google Cloud project, create storage buckets, and deploy cloud functions. You'll also need to know how to configure the Shopify API and handle Shopify events. If you're new to either platform, you may want to start with some basic tutorials and documentation to get familiar with the concepts and tools.

Integrating Shopify with Google Cloud can be a powerful way to build scalable and reliable Shopify apps. By leveraging the strengths of both platforms, you can create powerful workflows and applications that can help you grow your business and serve your customers better.

Integrating Shopify with Azure

Integrating Shopify with Azure

Azure is Microsoft's cloud computing platform that offers a wide range of services, including virtual machines, storage, and databases. Integrating Shopify with Azure can provide a scalable and secure hosting solution for your Shopify app.

To begin, you will need to create an Azure account and set up a virtual machine to host your Shopify app. You can choose from a variety of operating systems, including Windows or Linux, depending on your app's requirements.

Once your virtual machine is up and running, you can install and configure the necessary software for your Shopify app. This may include a web server, database, and other dependencies.

Next, you will need to set up a custom domain for your app using Azure's DNS service. This will allow you to use your own domain name instead of the default Azure domain.

To integrate your Shopify store with Azure, you can use Shopify's API to connect to your virtual machine. This will enable you to perform actions such as retrieving orders, updating products, and managing customers.

You can also use Azure's storage services to store and manage your app's data. This can include user data, product information, and other relevant data for your app.

To ensure the security of your app and its data, you can use Azure's security features, such as firewalls, encryption, and access controls. This will help protect your app from unauthorized access and data breaches.

Overall, integrating Shopify with Azure can provide a powerful and flexible hosting solution for your Shopify app. By leveraging Azure's cloud computing platform, you can ensure that your app is scalable, secure, and reliable.

Testing and Deployment

Introduction to Testing and Deployment

Introduction to Testing and Deployment

Testing and deployment are two critical aspects of software development. They play a significant role in ensuring that the application is working correctly and delivering the expected results. In this chapter, we will discuss the basics of testing and deployment and how they are essential for full-stack Shopify app development.

Testing

Testing is the process of verifying that the application is functioning correctly and meets the requirements. It involves checking the application for errors, bugs, and other issues that may affect its performance. Testing is a crucial part of the development process as it helps to identify problems early on and prevent them from becoming more significant issues later.

There are various types of testing that developers can perform, including unit testing, integration testing, and acceptance testing. Unit testing involves testing individual components of the application, such as functions or modules, to ensure that they are working correctly. Integration testing involves testing the interaction between different components to ensure that they are working together correctly. And acceptance testing involves testing the application as a whole to ensure that it meets the business requirements.

Deployment

Deployment is the process of releasing the application to the production environment. It involves transferring the application from the development environment to the server, configuring the server, and ensuring that the application is running correctly. Deployment is a crucial part of the development process as it determines whether the application will be able to handle the production load.

There are various deployment strategies that developers can use, including continuous deployment, blue-green deployment, and canary deployment. Continuous deployment involves deploying changes to the application as soon as they are made, ensuring that the application is always up-to-date. Blue-green deployment involves deploying two identical environments, with one environment serving as the production environment and the other as the staging environment. Canary deployment involves releasing the changes to a small group of users before releasing them to the entire user base.

Conclusion

In conclusion, testing and deployment are essential for full-stack Shopify app development. By testing the application thoroughly and deploying it correctly, developers can ensure that the application is functioning correctly and meets the business requirements. Testing and deployment are not only critical for the development process, but they also play a significant role in ensuring the success of the application in the production environment. Therefore, developers should pay close attention to testing and deployment to ensure that their application performs optimally.

Automated Testing for Shopify Apps

Automated Testing for Shopify Apps

Automated testing is an essential part of developing any software application, including Shopify apps. It helps to ensure that your app is functioning correctly and free of bugs that could impact its performance and functionality. Automated testing involves using specialized software tools to run tests on your application automatically, rather than manually.

One of the main benefits of automated testing is that it saves time and effort. Instead of manually testing each new feature or update, you can set up automated tests to run in the background, which can detect issues early on in the development process. This can help you to catch and fix bugs before they become more difficult and costly to resolve.

In addition to saving time and effort, automated testing can also improve the quality of your Shopify app. By running tests automatically, you can ensure that your app is functioning as intended across different devices, operating systems, and browsers. This can help to provide a better user experience for your customers and increase the overall satisfaction of your app.

There are several types of automated tests that you can use for your Shopify app, including unit tests, integration tests, and end-to-end tests. Unit tests are used to test individual components of your app, such as functions or methods. Integration tests are used to test how different parts of your app work together, while end-to-end tests are used to test the entire app from start to finish.

To set up automated testing for your Shopify app, you can use a variety of tools and frameworks, such as Selenium, Jest, Mocha, and Cypress. These tools allow you to write and run tests using popular programming languages like JavaScript and Python. You can also use Shopify's own testing framework, called Polaris, which is designed specifically for testing Shopify apps.

In conclusion, automated testing is an essential part of developing high-quality Shopify apps. By using specialized software tools and frameworks, you can save time and effort, improve the quality of your app, and provide a better user experience for your customers. Whether you're a beginner or an experienced Shopify app developer, automated testing is a technique that you should definitely consider incorporating into your development process.

Continuous Integration and Deployment

Continuous Integration and Deployment (CI/CD) is an essential part of modern software development. It is a practice where developers integrate their code changes into a shared repository multiple times a day. This process allows the development team to detect and fix issues early on, reducing the risk of bugs and errors in the final product. In this subchapter, we'll discuss how to implement CI/CD in the context of full-stack Shopify app development.

CI/CD in Full-stack Shopify App Development

In full-stack Shopify app development, CI/CD plays a crucial role in ensuring that the app is of high quality, stable, and reliable. The process involves the following steps:

1. Code Integration: Developers merge their code changes into a shared repository. This step ensures that the code is up-to-date, and there are no conflicts between different developers' changes.

2. Build Automation: The code is built automatically, and the build process is tested to ensure that it works correctly. Any errors or issues are identified in this step.

3. Testing and Quality Assurance: Automated tests are run to ensure that the app's functionality works as expected. Testing can include unit tests, integration tests, and end-to-end tests. The quality of the code is also checked to ensure that it meets the required standards.

4. Deployment: The built and tested code is deployed automatically to the production environment. This step ensures that the app is available to the users as soon as possible.

Benefits of CI/CD in Full-stack Shopify App Development

CI/CD provides several benefits in full-stack Shopify app development, including:

1. Faster Time-to-Market: CI/CD enables developers to release new features and updates quickly and frequently. This approach allows the app to stay up-to-date with the latest changes in the market.

2. Better Quality: Automated testing and quality assurance ensure that the app is of high quality and meets the required standards.

3. Reduced Risk: CI/CD reduces the risk of bugs and errors in the final product. Early detection and fixing of issues ensure that the app is stable and reliable.

Conclusion

CI/CD is an essential practice in full-stack Shopify app development. It ensures that the app is of high quality, stable, and reliable. By implementing CI/CD, developers can release new features and updates quickly and frequently, reducing the time-to-market and improving the overall quality of the app.

Shopify App Deployment Best Practices

Shopify App Deployment Best Practices

Deploying a Shopify app is a critical step in the development process, and it requires careful consideration of several factors. In this section, we will discuss some best practices for deploying Shopify apps.

1. Test the app thoroughly before deployment

Before deploying the app, it is essential to test it thoroughly. This includes testing the app's functionality, user interface, and performance. You should also test the app on different devices and browsers to ensure it works correctly on all platforms.

2. Use a staging environment for testing

It is recommended to use a staging environment to test the app before deploying it to the production environment. This will allow you to test the app without affecting the live site. You can also use the staging environment to test different scenarios and edge cases.

3. Use a version control system

Using a version control system like Git is essential when deploying Shopify apps. It allows you to track changes and revert to previous versions if necessary. It also makes it easier to collaborate with other developers and manage different versions of the app.

4. Ensure security and data protection

Security and data protection are critical factors when deploying Shopify apps. You should ensure that the app is secure and complies with Shopify's security requirements. You should also protect user data and ensure that it is not exposed to unauthorized parties.

5. Optimize the app for performance

Optimizing the app for performance is essential for a good user experience. You should optimize the app's code, images, and other assets to ensure fast loading times. You should also test the app's performance on different devices and networks to ensure it works well under different conditions.

6. Provide clear documentation

Clear documentation is essential when deploying Shopify apps. You should provide documentation that outlines the app's functionality, installation steps, and troubleshooting tips. This will help users install and use the app correctly and reduce the number of support requests.

In conclusion, deploying a Shopify app requires careful consideration of several factors. By following these best practices, you can ensure that your app is secure, optimized, and easy to use.

Conclusion

Recap of Full-Stack Shopify App Development

In this chapter, we will be recapping the key concepts and technologies that we have learned throughout this book in regards to Full-Stack Shopify App Development.

At the beginning of the book, we covered the basics of Shopify development, including how to create a Shopify app and how to set up a development environment. From there, we delved into the world of Full-Stack development, where we explored different front-end technologies such as React and Vue.js, and how to integrate them with Shopify's APIs.

We also discussed the importance of server-side development and how to build a custom Shopify app using Node.js and GraphQL. We learned how to authenticate app requests, use webhooks to receive real-time notifications, and how to secure the app using various security measures.

Next, we covered the topic of Shopify app deployment, where we learned how to deploy Shopify apps to the cloud using platforms such as Heroku and AWS. We also explored different deployment strategies, such as continuous integration and delivery, and how to automate the deployment process using tools like Travis CI.

Lastly, we discussed how to optimize Shopify app performance and scalability, and how to monitor and debug the app using tools like New Relic and Loggly. We also learned how to handle errors and exceptions, and how to implement caching to improve app performance.

Overall, this book provided a comprehensive guide to Full-Stack Shopify app development, covering everything from user interface design to cloud integration. We hope that this recap has helped you to review and solidify your understanding of the key concepts and technologies covered in this book, and that you are now well-equipped to develop your own Full-Stack Shopify apps.

Future Trends in Shopify App Development

As the e-commerce industry continues to grow and evolve, so too does the demand for innovative and user-friendly Shopify apps. As developers, it's important to stay ahead of the curve and anticipate future trends in Shopify app development in order to create apps that will remain relevant and useful for years to come.

One trend that is sure to shape the future of Shopify app development is the increasing importance of mobile optimization. With more and more consumers shopping on their mobile devices, it's essential that Shopify apps are designed with mobile users in mind. This means creating apps that are responsive, fast, and easy to use on smaller screens.

Another trend to watch out for is the rise of artificial intelligence and machine learning. These technologies can be used to personalize the shopping experience for individual customers, making it easier for them to find the products they're looking for and increasing the likelihood of a sale. Developers who are able to incorporate AI and machine learning into their Shopify apps will be well-positioned to succeed in the future.

Cloud integration is also becoming increasingly important in the world of e-commerce. Shopify apps that are able to seamlessly integrate with popular cloud platforms like Amazon Web Services and Google Cloud will be in high demand, as merchants look for ways to streamline their operations and improve their bottom line.

Finally, it's worth noting that the future of Shopify app development is likely to be heavily influenced by the ongoing COVID-19 pandemic. As more consumers shift their shopping habits online, there will be a growing need for apps that can help merchants adapt to this new reality. Developers who are able to create apps that address the unique challenges of the current environment will be well-positioned to succeed in the coming years.

In conclusion, the future of Shopify app development is bright, but it's important for developers to stay ahead of the curve and anticipate future trends in order to create apps that will remain relevant and useful for years to come. By focusing on mobile optimization, AI and machine learning, cloud integration, and the unique challenges of the COVID-19 pandemic, developers can create apps that will help merchants thrive in the ever-changing world of e-commerce.

Additional Resources for Full-Stack Shopify App Development

As a developer working on full-stack Shopify app development, it's important to have access to a variety of resources that can help you create robust and efficient applications. In this subchapter, we'll explore some of the top resources available to help you take your Shopify app development to the next level.

1. Shopify App Store: The Shopify App Store is a great place to start when looking for resources to help with your full-stack app development. Here, you'll find a wide range of apps and tools that can help you streamline your development process, improve your app's functionality, and connect with other developers in the Shopify community.

2. Shopify API Documentation: The Shopify API documentation is an invaluable resource for developers working on full-stack app development. This comprehensive guide provides detailed information on Shopify's APIs, including how to use them effectively and best practices for integration. It's a must-read for any developer working on Shopify app development.

3. Shopify Partners Program: The Shopify Partners Program is designed to help developers, designers, and other professionals grow their businesses by working with Shopify. As a member of the program, you'll have access to a variety of resources, including educational materials, marketing support, and technical resources to help you develop and launch your apps.

4. Shopify Meetups and Events: Attending Shopify meetups and events is a great way to connect with other developers and learn more about the latest trends and best practices in full-stack app development. You'll have the opportunity to network with other industry professionals, attend workshops and presentations, and get hands-on experience with new tools and technologies.

5. Online Learning Resources: There are many online learning resources available to help you improve your full-stack Shopify app development skills. Platforms like Udemy, Coursera, and Skillshare offer courses and tutorials on everything from basic Shopify app development to advanced topics like cloud integration and data analytics.

In conclusion, as a developer working on full-stack Shopify app development, it's important to take advantage of all available resources to improve your skills and create successful apps. By using the resources listed above, you'll be well on your way to becoming a top-notch Shopify app developer.

Final Thoughts.

Final Thoughts

As you come to the end of this book, you should feel confident in your ability to develop full-stack Shopify apps. You have learned how to create user interfaces that are both functional and visually appealing. You have also learned how to integrate your app with Shopify's cloud infrastructure, allowing your app to interact with Shopify's data and services.

But developing a full-stack Shopify app is more than just knowing how to code. It requires an understanding of the Shopify platform and its ecosystem. It also requires a deep understanding of your users' needs and behaviors.

As you continue to develop your app, keep in mind the following best practices:

1. Keep it simple: Avoid overcomplicating your app. Focus on the core features that your users need and make sure they are easy to use.

2. Test, test, test: Test your app thoroughly before releasing it to the public. Make sure it works on all devices and browsers.

3. Listen to your users: Pay attention to feedback from your users. Use their feedback to improve your app and add new features.

4. Stay up to date: Keep up to date with the latest trends and technologies in full-stack Shopify app development. Attend conferences, read blogs, and stay active in the developer community.

5. Collaborate: Collaborate with other developers and designers to create the best possible app. This can help you see your app from different perspectives and improve its overall quality.

Remember, developing a full-stack Shopify app is a journey, not a destination. There will always be room for improvement and new features to add. But with the knowledge and skills you have gained from this book, you are well on your way to creating successful and innovative apps for the Shopify platform.